Douglas MacArthur

History Maker Bios

Stephanie Sammartino McPherson

LERNER PUBLICATIONS COMPANY • MINNEAPOLIS

To Major Angelo J. Sammartino, USMC, Ret., veteran of Guadalcanal and the Korean War, and to Marion R. Sammartino, who waited and bravely took care of the home front

Special thanks to my editor, Carol Hinz, for her help and astute comments; to my father, Angelo Sammartino, for reading this manuscript and sharing his personal experiences; and to my husband, Richard Mcpherson, for his suggestions and never-failing support

Illustrations by Tim Parlin

Text copyright © 2005 by Stephanie Sammartino Mcpherson
Illustrations copyright © 2005 by Lerner Publications Company

Lerner Publications Company
A division of Lerner Publishing Group
241 First Avenue North
Minneapolis, MN 55401 U.S.A.

Website address: www.lernerbooks.com

Library of Congress Cataloging-in-Publication Data

McPherson, Stephanie Sammartino.
    Douglas MacArthur / by Stephanie Sammartino McPherson.
        p.   cm. — (History maker bios)
    Includes bibliographical references and index.
    ISBN: 0–8225–2434–1 (lib. bdg. : alk. paper)
    1. MacArthur, Douglas, 1880–1964—Juvenile literature. 2. Generals—United States—Biography—Juvenile literature. 3. United States. Army—Biography—Juvenile literature. 4. United States—History, Military—20th century—Juvenile literature. I. Title. II. Series.
    E745.M3M38 2005
    355'0.0092—dc22   2004002418

Manufactured in the United States of America
1 2 3 4 5 6 – JR – 10 09 08 07 06 05

TABLE OF CONTENTS

INTRODUCTION

Douglas MacArthur always wanted to be a soldier. He dreamed of battles that would make him a war hero, just like his father.

In World War I (1914–1918), Douglas was a brave leader in Europe. The army made him one of the nation's youngest generals. Years later, Douglas helped win World War II (1939–1945). His courage inspired many soldiers.

When World War II ended, Douglas hoped for a better, safer world. He helped rebuild Japan into a peaceful nation.

But there were still battles to fight. Douglas was called to fight for freedom in the Korean War (1950–1953). He won an important victory and was called a military genius.

This is his story.

THE MATERIAL OF A SOLDIER

Douglas MacArthur grew up surrounded by soldiers. He was born at a U.S. Army base in Arkansas on January 26, 1880. His family soon moved to a fort in New Mexico. As a baby, Douglas heard the noises of the military all around him—the bugle calls, the loud footsteps of marching men, and the sound of gunshots.

Douglas's father, Captain Arthur MacArthur, helped protect settlers in the southwestern United States from attacks by Native Americans. Douglas's mother, Pinky, kept very busy taking care of her small sons, Douglas and older brothers Malcolm and Arthur.

When Douglas was four years old, his father's soldiers marched three hundred miles to Fort Seldon, New Mexico. Douglas took his turn marching at the front of the line. He was proud to do his duty just like a real soldier.

From the time Douglas was a young boy, he admired his father, Captain Arthur MacArthur (LEFT).

Life at Fort Seldon offered everything an adventure-loving boy could want. Douglas learned to ride a horse and shoot a gun even before he could read and write! Fort Seldon did not have a school nearby, so Pinky MacArthur taught her sons herself. Every night at bedtime, she reminded Douglas, "You must grow up to be a great man."

CIVIL WAR HERO

Douglas's favorite war story was about his own father. During the Civil War (1861–1865), Captain MacArthur had stuffed a bunch of letters in his shirt. A bullet struck him right at that spot, tearing through the paper. But the letters slowed the bullet just enough to save his life. Every time visitors came to the fort, a proud Douglas urged his father, "Show them the letters."

Douglas, the young man with the number on his jersey, was an athlete at West Texas Military Academy.

Like all military families, the MacArthurs moved often. In Fort Leavenworth, Kansas, and in Washington, D.C., Douglas went to regular schools. He didn't do as well as his parents would have liked. But at the age of thirteen, Douglas heard his father say, "I think there is the material of a soldier in that boy." Douglas was thrilled.

Not long afterwards, the MacArthurs moved to San Antonio, Texas. At the West Texas Military Academy, Douglas suddenly found his studies fascinating. He was the top student in his class. He also played football, baseball, and tennis.

When Douglas graduated in 1897, he wanted to go to West Point, the country's top army college. But to get into the school, he had to be chosen by a congressman or the president of the United States.

Pinky had an idea. She and Douglas moved to Milwaukee, Wisconsin, where she knew the local congressman, Theobald Otjen. Pinky hoped that Douglas would win a special competition making him that congressman's candidate to West Point.

This photo of Douglas's mother, Pinky, was taken in 1875, before Douglas was born.

The night before the exam, Douglas was too nervous to sleep. In the morning, he felt sick. "Doug," said his mother quietly, "you'll win if you don't lose your nerve."

Somehow Douglas managed to keep his nerve. He received the top score and, one year later, set off to West Point in New York State.

2 RISING THROUGH THE RANKS

Douglas worked hard at West Point. He finished first in his class on June 11, 1903. He was twenty-three years old and a second lieutenant in the army. Soon Douglas was moving from place to place just as he had as a child. He even received orders to join his father on a tour of eastern Asia and Japan.

At the age of twenty-three, Douglas was second lieutenant in the army.

From Japan, Douglas went to a military school in Washington, D.C. While there, he became a military assistant to President Theodore Roosevelt. His duties were routine. But Douglas found life in the White House exciting.

In 1908, Douglas was sent to Fort Leavenworth, Kansas. He was placed in charge of Company K. It was the lowest ranked of twenty-one companies at the fort. Douglas made his men work very hard, and he always praised them for doing a good job.

At the next inspection, Company K was ranked number one. "I could not have been happier if they had made me a general," Douglas said.

But Douglas was very happy when he became a captain in 1911. About two years later, he was selected as a member of the General Staff of the army in Washington, D.C. Thirty-three-year-old Douglas worked with some of the nation's top officers.

In 1917, the United States entered World War I, which had broken out three years earlier in Europe. The army desperately needed more fighting men.

U.S. soldiers take aim from snow-covered trenches in December 1917.

WORLD WAR I

When a German submarine sank the British ship *Lusitania*, more than one hundred Americans lost their lives. On April 6, 1917, the U.S. Congress declared war on Germany. The United States joined the Allied powers, which included France, Russia, and Great Britain. They fought the Central powers of Germany, Austria-Hungary, Bulgaria, and Turkey.

Douglas believed that the National Guard could help. This special force is made up of state units trained to keep order in time of crisis. Douglas wanted to combine men from different states into one fighting unit. He said that it would "stretch over the whole country like a rainbow." Most people in the War Department didn't like the idea. But President Woodrow Wilson did. To Douglas's surprise, he was promoted so that he could help lead the Rainbow Division to fight in France.

3 TESTED IN BATTLE

No one had ever seen a military leader quite like Douglas. The other senior officers spent more time planning battles than fighting them. They were supposed to stay away from the action and focus on the big picture. In France, Douglas wanted to get as close to the fighting as possible.

Douglas also stood out because of his style of dress. He refused to wear a helmet or a gas mask—although he made sure his troops wore them. Instead of a regular uniform, he wore a turtleneck sweater, riding pants, a flattened cap, and a long purple scarf knit by his mother. He even carried a riding crop instead of his gun!

Douglas, shown in France in 1918, ignored army uniform rules.

Douglas was very lucky in battle. One night, he led a small group into enemy territory to learn where German defenses were weakest. A sudden burst of enemy fire sent the soldiers running for the nearest places to hide. Afterward, Douglas discovered he was the only one left alive. Douglas's information about the Germans' weak point helped the troops take over an important enemy post.

By the end of the war in 1918, Douglas had become one of the youngest generals in the army. He had also earned seven Silver Stars for bravery.

Soldiers in France run for cover during a World War I battle.

Douglas ran the U.S. Military Academy at West Point for four years.

Back in the United States, Douglas was put in charge of West Point. Immediately, he made changes so that the students, called cadets, would get the best education possible. He also made sure that all cadets had a chance to play sports.

In 1922, the army sent Douglas to the Philippines to lead U.S. troops based there. Douglas brought his new wife, Louise, and his two stepchildren with him to Manila, the capital of the Philippines.

Douglas was happy with the job, but Louise missed the United States. She felt happier when Douglas was sent to Baltimore, Maryland. But in 1928, Douglas was sent back to the Philippines. Soon after, Louise and Douglas were divorced.

Less than two years later, Douglas became chief of staff of the entire army. He moved to Washington, D.C. When Douglas's term as chief of staff ended, he went back to the Philippines by boat.

THE PHILIPPINES

The Philippines are a group of islands in the Pacific Ocean. For most of the 1800s, Spain ruled the islands. At the end of the Spanish-American War in 1898, the United States took control of the islands. U.S. troops occupied the islands to help rule the country and protect the people. The United States planned to make the Philippines independent in the early 1940s.

Douglas married Jean Faircloth (RIGHT) on April 30, 1937.

During the trip, he met a woman named Jean Marie Faircloth. After they reached Manila, Douglas and Jean saw each other almost every day. In 1937, they were married. Their son Arthur was born in February 1938.

Douglas loved spending time with his son. Every morning, Douglas and Arthur marched around the bedroom yelling, "Boom, boom, boomity boom!" Afterward, they sang songs while Douglas shaved.

The Japanese bombed Pearl Harbor in a surprise attack on December 7, 1941.

In 1941, President Franklin Delano Roosevelt made Douglas the commander of all the U.S. forces in the Far East. Like the president, Douglas worried that Japan was planning to take over many islands in the Pacific Ocean. Douglas spent most of his time working on a plan to protect the Philippines.

But Japan struck before Douglas was ready. On December 7, 1941, the Japanese bombed Pearl Harbor, a U.S. Navy base in Hawaii. Douglas was shocked.

Within hours, Japan turned its attention to the Philippines. Japanese aircraft attacked the U.S. Army's airfield and destroyed most of the planes on the ground. Less than three weeks later, the Japanese invaded the beaches and marched toward Manila. Douglas didn't have enough soldiers to stop them. On Christmas Eve, Douglas, Jean, and three-year-old Arthur escaped from the city by boat.

4 LET EVERY ARM BE STEELED

On December 26, Douglas acted to keep Manila safe. He declared it an "open city." This meant that Douglas would not try to defend the city. The Japanese would have no reason to attack and destroy it.

Douglas set up his new command on the island of Corregidor, about twenty miles from Manila. Soon the Japanese found out where he was and attacked the island with airplanes. Jean and little Arthur hurried into a shelter. But Douglas stayed outside without even wearing a helmet. He wanted to set an example of bravery for his men.

Manila was a bustling city just twenty miles from Douglas's new command on Corregidor.

Douglas had his military office in an underground tunnel. But he continued to stand outdoors during even the worst air attacks. He knew his troops couldn't defeat the Japanese without help from the United States. He needed food, bullets, airplanes, and men as soon as possible. President Roosevelt promised help, but nothing arrived. Douglas expected to die on Corregidor. Jean bravely said she and Arthur would stay with him no matter what happened.

WORLD WAR II

In declaring war on Japan, the United States also entered the war in Europe. Led by Adolf Hitler, Germany had joined forces with Italy and Japan. These counries formed the Axis powers. Great Britain, France, the Soviet Union, and the United States, worked together as the Allied powers.

The U.S. Congress awarded Douglas the Medal of Honor for his bravery in the Philippines.

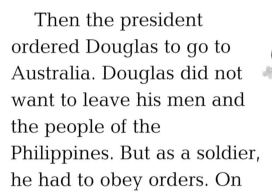

Then the president ordered Douglas to go to Australia. Douglas did not want to leave his men and the people of the Philippines. But as a soldier, he had to obey orders. On

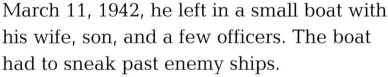

March 11, 1942, he left in a small boat with his wife, son, and a few officers. The boat had to sneak past enemy ships.

When Douglas arrived in Australia, he said, "The President of the United States ordered me to break through the Japanese lines. I came through and I shall return." Douglas's dangerous escape and his bold words amazed Americans. He was celebrated as a hero and was awarded the Medal of Honor.

Not long after Douglas arrived in Australia, the Philippines surrendered to Japan. Douglas wanted the United States to free the islands as soon as possible. But military leaders in Washington, D.C., disagreed.

During the war, Douglas shared his thoughts with aides and visitors. Walking back and forth, he talked on and on. One aide said that Douglas paced about five miles a day!

Douglas, shortly after arriving in Australia, in March 1942

The United States' Avenger bombers attack Japan.

Douglas helped lead Allied troops to stop the Japanese from attacking Port Moresby in New Guinea. This win ruined Japan's plans to attack Australia. Then Douglas sought to free South Pacific islands that had been taken over by the Japanese.

Douglas decided to strike at the enemy's weakest positions. That way, his troops could win battles without losing a lot of men. U.S. soldiers took over airfields or built new ones. They used airplane attacks to keep food and supplies from getting through to the stronger Japanese bases. This plan worked to regain many islands.

Douglas (SECOND FROM RIGHT) wades to the shore at Leyte.

Two and a half years passed before
Douglas returned to the Philippines.
During a fierce battle, he approached the
island of Leyte in the Philippines. He
made sure his landing craft headed where
the fighting was heaviest. "People of the
Philippines, I have returned," he
announced. He told them to be brave,
saying, "Let no heart be faint. Let every
arm be steeled." By December 1944, the
Allied soldiers controlled all of Leyte.

When U.S. troops reached Manila, the Japanese fought desperately. The beautiful city that Douglas had saved earlier was badly damaged. Douglas watched flames sweep through his former home at the top of the Manila Hotel.

After winning back the Philippines, Douglas and the Allies still had to defeat Japan. U.S. leaders wanted to avoid a long, difficult fight that would cause thousands of Americans to die. Instead of sending more troops, the United States dropped two atomic bombs. One fell on the Japanese city of Hiroshima, the other on Nagasaki. The damage was overwhelming. More than 200,000 people were killed. Days later, on August 14, 1945, Japan stopped fighting.

A huge, mushroom-shaped cloud rises from the atomic bomb dropped on Nagasaki, Japan.

Japan officially surrendered to Douglas on September 2, 1945, aboard the USS *Missouri*. It was the largest battleship among more than 250 that crammed Tokyo Bay. During the surrender ceremony, Douglas said, "Let us pray that peace be now restored to the world and that God will preserve it always." The Japanese diplomats on the ship hoped for peace as well.

Japanese diplomats stand ready for the official surrender on September 2, 1945.

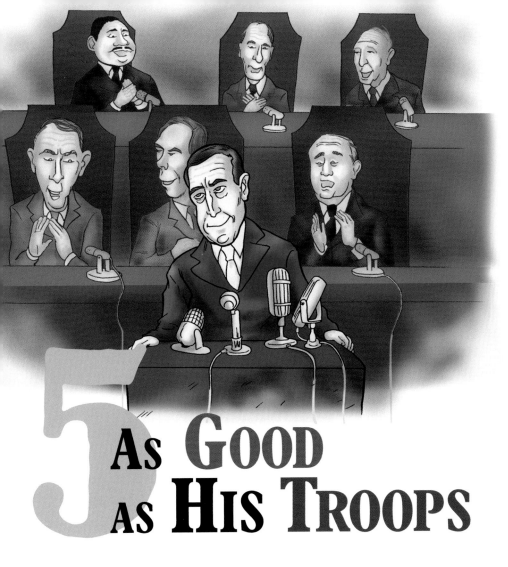

5 AS GOOD AS HIS TROOPS

Douglas's trust of the Japanese people helped him as he started his next task. He had to help Japan become a safe, stable country. It was a huge responsibility.

Douglas and Emperor Hirohito both signed this photo of their meeting in September 1945.

At that time, an emperor ruled Japan. Shortly after Japan's surrender, Emperor Hirohito came to visit Douglas. Very few Americans had ever met the emperor. Jean was so curious about the meeting that she hid behind a curtain to listen. The emperor took full responsibility for everything Japan had done during the war. Douglas was very impressed.

Douglas moved into the U.S. Embassy in Tokyo, Japan's capital. It had been badly damaged by bombing. But the rest of the city was in even worse shape. Everywhere Douglas looked, he saw rubble and wreckage. All over the country, people were starving. Douglas decided to give the Japanese people thousands of tons of food. The food would have gone to U.S. soldiers if the war had continued. Douglas's decision upset some members of the U.S. Congress.

But Douglas was firm. He could not help the country if the people were hungry.

Much of Tokyo was destroyed by bombing during World War II.

Under Douglas's leadership, Japanese citizens and businesses gained new freedom. They could act without government control. Women received the right to vote. Most important, a new constitution was adopted. It took power from the emperor and gave it to the people.

Douglas worked hard every day, even on weekends and holidays. He became very popular in Japan. Hundreds of people waited quietly each day to watch Douglas enter and leave his office building.

Japanese citizens gather to show their support for Douglas (RIGHT, ON STAIRS).

Showing Respect

Every morning when Douglas drove to his office in Tokyo, he passed a street sweeper. To show respect, the street sweeper turned his back as Douglas's car passed by. That's how the Japanese people treated the emperor. They were not supposed to look at him directly. Douglas didn't like this custom at all. One day, he stopped the car. He asked his aide, who spoke Japanese, to explain that people in the United States greet each other face-to-face. After that, the street sweeper always faced Douglas as he drove by.

Almost five years after starting his job in Japan, Douglas had to turn his attention toward another country—Korea. At the end of World War II, Korea had been divided in two. North Koreans and South Koreans wanted to form one country, but they could not agree on what type of government to have. South Korea wanted democracy, but North Korea wanted Communism.

President Truman (LEFT) chose Douglas to lead U.S. troops during the Korean War.

In Communist countries, everything is owned by the government. Freedom of speech is often not allowed. On June 25, 1950, North Korean Communists invaded South Korea. President Harry Truman put seventy-year-old Douglas in charge of U.S. troops to push back the Communists.

Soon other countries joined the fight. Douglas was made commander of all of these forces. The situation was bad until Douglas came up with a bold and dangerous plan. He decided to attack the port of Inchon, well behind enemy lines. This move would block the North Koreans from getting supplies.

Army officials in Washington, D.C., were worried. But Douglas felt sure of victory at Inchon and predicted the action would save 100,000 lives.

On September 15, 1950, Douglas watched the attack. Bullets rained down as his boat approached the shore of an island. But he refused to move to safety. The landing at Inchon was a brilliant success. Within two weeks, Douglas's troops had recaptured the Korean capital of Seoul and pushed the Communists back over the boundary into North Korea.

Douglas, holding binoculars, watches as his troops attack Inchon.

Douglas inspects troops at an airfield in South Korea on February 21, 1951.

The war wasn't over. Chinese Communists began to help the North Koreans. Douglas wanted to win even though it meant crossing from North Korea into China. But President Truman and other top military commanders feared it would lead to war with China. When Douglas disagreed with Truman in public, the president was furious. On April 10, 1951, he fired Douglas.

But Douglas was still wildly popular—
both in Japan and the United States. On his
way home, he stopped in Tokyo. Hundreds
of thousands of Japanese citizens filled the
streets to say good-bye. Days later, Douglas
was back in Washington, D.C., speaking
to Congress. Every few
minutes, cheers and
applause drowned
out his voice.

Douglas is
welcomed as a hero
in New York City.

Douglas, Jean, and thirteen-year-old Arthur moved into an apartment in New York City. Douglas became chairman of a large company. Through the years, three presidents welcomed his visits to the White House. Douglas spent his free time enjoying football and plays and visiting with his friends.

Douglas celebrated his eighty-fourth birthday on January 26, 1964.

When Douglas MacArthur died on April 5, 1964, people all over the country praised him as one of the best soldiers of the century. Douglas had always enjoyed the spotlight, but he had a more modest version of his success. "A general is just as good or just as bad as the troops under his command make him," he said when he was eighty-two years old. "Mine were great."

TIMELINE

DOUGLAS MACARTHUR
WAS BORN ON JANUARY
26, 1880.

In the year . . .

1883   Douglas's brother Malcolm died.

1903   Douglas graduated from West Point.   Age 23

1912   he became a member of the army's General Staff.

1914   World War I began in Europe.

1917   the Rainbow Division was formed from the National Guard.   Age 37

1922   he married Louise Brooks on Valentine's Day.
he went to the Philippines.

1929   he and Louise were divorced.
he was sent once more to the Philippines.

1930   he was appointed chief of staff of the army.   Age 50

1937   he married Jean Marie Faircloth.

1938   his son Arthur IV was born.

1941   on December 7, the Japanese bombed Pearl Harbor.   Age 61

1942   Douglas was named commander of Allied forces in the southwest Pacific.
he left the Philippines for Australia.

1944   he liberated the Philippines from the Japanese.

1945   the United States dropped atomic bombs on two Japanese cities.
he assumed the leadership of occupied Japan.   Age 65

1950   he became commander of U.S. and international forces in Korea.   Age 70

1951   he was fired by President Harry S. Truman.

1964   Douglas died on April 5.

Bringing Home the Gold

Douglas MacArthur always loved sports. In 1927, he was thrilled to serve as president of the U.S. Olympic Committee. The games took place in 1928 in Amsterdam. Douglas enjoyed meeting Queen Wilhelmina of Holland and encouraging the U.S. athletes to do their best. He wanted to bring home lots of medals.

Sometimes Douglas had to deal with touchy situations. The manager of the boxing team felt a poor decision had been made in one of the contests. He wanted his athletes to quit the rest of the competition in protest. Douglas spoke to the athletes as if they were soldiers. "Americans never quit," he declared. "We are here to represent the greatest country on earth. We did not come here to lose gracefully. We came here to win."

Douglas's pep talk must have paid off. No other country came close to the United States' performance. The U.S. teams set seventeen new Olympic records and won more medals than any other country.

This poster was designed for the 1928 Olympics.

FURTHER READING

NONFICTION

Morimoto, Junko. *My Hiroshima.* New York: Viking, 1990. This is a first-person account of a child's experience of the dropping of the atomic bomb. As an adult, Morimoto returned to a peaceful Hiroshima.

Panchyk, Richard. *World War II for Kids: A History with 21 Activities.* Chicago: Chicago Review Press, 2002. First-person accounts of the war are included as well as directions for such activities as writing a patriotic song, interviewing a veteran, and making a bandage.

Shuter, Jane. *War Machines: Military Vehicles Past and Present.* Chicago: Raintree, 2004. This book describes war machines from ancient chariots through modern, computerized vehicles. Large illustrations accompany the simple text.

Young, Jeff C. *The Korean War.* Berkeley Heights, NJ: MyReportLinks.com Books, 2003. From battles to weapons, this book describes all aspects of the Korean War.

FICTION

Kudlinski, Kathleen V. *Pearl Harbor Is Burning! A Story of World War II.* New York: Viking Penguin, 1991. The bombing of Pearl Harbor tests the friendship of Frank, a newcomer to Hawaii, and Kenji, a Japanese American boy.

Tripp, Valerie. *Meet Molly: An American Girl.* Madison, WI: Pleasant Co., 1986. Molly's father leaves to fight in World War II, and the family has to make many changes.

WEBSITES

The Douglas MacArthur Memorial
http://www.MacArthurMemorial.org/ This website
describes the museum, special exhibits, and programs of
the MacArthur Memorial in Norfolk, Virginia.

Congressional Medal of Honor
http://www.medalofhonor.com/DouglasMacArthur.htm
This site discusses MacArthur's military decorations and
provides links to letters, speeches, and documents.

SELECT BIBLIOGRAPHY

BOOKS
Blair, Clay, Jr. *MacArthur.* Garden City, NY: Doubleday, 1977.

Egeberg, Roger Olaf. *The General: MacArthur and the Man
He Called "Doc."* New York: Hippocrene Books, 1983.

James, D. Clayton. *The Years of MacArthur.* 3 vols. Boston:
Houghton Mifflin Company, 1970–1985.

MacArthur, Douglas. *Reminiscences.* New York: McGraw-
Hill, 1964.

Manchester, William. *American Caesar: Douglas
MacArthur, 1880–1964.* Boston: Little, Brown, 1978.

Perret, Geoffrey. *Old Soldiers Never Die: The Life of
Douglas MacArthur.* New York: Random House, 1996.

TRANSCRIPTS
"Enhanced Transcript." *American Experience: MacArthur.*
http://www.pbs.org/wgbh/amex/macarthur/filmmore
/transcript/index.html (accessed August 2, 2004).

INDEX

Acknowledgments

For photographs and artwork: MacArthur Memorial, pp. 4, 7, 9, 10, 13, 17, 19, 21, 34, 36, 41, 42; © Underwood & Underwood/CORBIS, p. 14; © CORBIS, p. 18; Library of Congress, pp. 22, 27 (LC-USW36-952); © Time Life Pictures/Getty Images, p. 25; © Hulton-Deutsch Collection/CORBIS, p. 28; National Archives, pp. 29, 30, 31, 32, 39, 40; © Bettmann/CORBIS, p. 35; U.S. Army/Courtesy of the Harry S. Truman Library, p. 38; © Leonard de Selva/CORBIS, p. 45. **Front cover:** © Getty Images. **Back cover:** MacArthur Memorial.

For quoted material: pp. 8, 9, 21, 43, 45, William Manchester, *American Caesar: Douglas MacArthur, 1880–1964* (Boston: Little, Brown, 1978); pp. 11, 14, 15, 32, Douglas MacArthur, *Reminiscences* (New York: McGraw-Hill, 1964); p. 27, Geoffrey Perret, *Old Soldiers Never Die: The Life of Douglas MacArthur* (New York: Random House, 1996); p. 30, "Enhanced Transcript," *American Experience: MacArthur,* http://www.pbs.org/wgbh/amex/macarthur/filmmore/transcript/ transcript3.html (accessed August 23, 2004).